A Whim

Ashia Solete

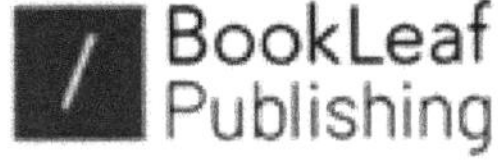

BookLeaf
Publishing

Presentation by *BookLeaf Publishing*

Web: www.bookleafpub.com

E-mail: info@bookleafpub.com

ISBN: 9789357210126

First edition 2022

DEDICATION

To Cookie

Basic Happenings

Returned from Bullis like a bulldog
Tail wagging, spazzing for that first class
Front row seats
Tongue lapping information before formation
began
Still haven't caught yoga
But a stretch might see after ordered to rest easy
Not as easy as Tee Karen's last briefing,
    but I'm sure we'll meet again
With Constance on the up and up I shall hydrate
in their honor
Water every heart with flowery words so their
jungle may be filled with color
Color me bad
A mad dog in the jungle
I am heated with this thick coat,
    but its covered me well
In wellness I share

Crook

So,
You say your cheeks hurt from smiling so hard
Don't think I have ever spotted a crook I'd like to
see again until I met you
Let us just say my heart hurt because my head
hard and I'd like to steal some comfort with you
I ain't that bad at bad things
And getting better
While staying on topic, why are you smiling
Don't say it is 'cause of me because only the
devil is a liar
So Goddess, tell me the ugly truth

Make-Up

Siphon off every nuisance, indulge in all the
pleasure
Climbing to the top,
   I want you where you want and settled
Come down only at your leisure
That connection where there's no such thing as I
can't kiss you
You mad, but *MWAH* I'm still here
Or I'm still heated after a 9 to 5 beating
MWAH
Ready to make a snack, take a nap, reactivate for
approach again
Embody the reproach 'cause that hot potato
tossing blame in your favor just ain't my type of
hype
Only thing right for a break up is the butterflies
fighting in your tummy
I'd cuddle you to pieces lovely

Effort Effect

I am pretty sure it's an apple a day keeps the doc
at bay
...and I'm screaming SCREW apple, you can owl
me if it's real
Visit if it's the realest you ever felt
Your presence has been the only thing to make
my heart melt
In a long time, a really long time
Choking on thoughts formerly collected dust in
my mind
Should I take it as a sign?
I'm choking already
Hurting you hasn't happened but I'm regretting
already
Ain't been resting well lately
I been questioning maybe
   this could all be a dream
We both grown enough to know plans don't
always sow accordingly to seams
But I'll suit up for you
Lace my sole up for you
Go toe to toe, broke for broke
Long as my home is with you

Foilage, That's Foul

5

I'm just a forget-me-not, locked in a safe box

Duplicity

6

Wasn't looking for an angel, one just fell in my
lap
My eyes only grazed you, should've known it
was a trap--in a trance
Sun strands, swimming across skin
Each stroke like kinfolk, just tryna move in

Don't Get Got, Get Em

The mini triumph after killing a spry roach
Apart from the men in black at the end of his last
rope
Reaching out for hope 'cause you know what
lurks in the darkness
Or rather what shimmers along the outskirts
No one likes tip toeing in dirty waters
'Til crossing borders the only options to move
forward
Keep your hands clean, been taught since
kindergarten
Yet mud under nails due to lessons life has to
offer
No scratching out of coffins or interesting verses
with a gopher
Just choices that go SPLAT or opportunities that
go golden

Take A Little and Do A Lot

Never raised to be afraid of work
Take a spoon of dirt and make goldmine worth
Coming from the Earth, nurture is my nature
Grew up with the flavor
Meet the last of the Mohicans
Babygirl got all she want plus everything she
needed
Poppa with allowances and Momma always
feeding
Cuzzo can be confided in and brothers always
keeping
Differences a split,
   but backs were covered against the demons
People think you got a lot, but looks can be
deceiving
Keep the substance out of objects,
   there's better things to believe in
Momma preach we all we got
Glad I finally stop to think she trippin'

Grasp

9

I have had kisses melt in my pocket

Ethical Egg

Hatched plans by a bad batch of man, oh man
  who gave them the upper hand in this
Land of the free still catching while they can
Stay glued to the media, it's all about having
fans
Young cats remain close to the heater from pots
to pan,
  can you handle
Woe is there to witness tears clash upon callous
hands
Who's to hold all the sorrow?
While the stomach disposes of all the Xans it
borrowed
The kitchen table stares blank

Velvet Punch

I was once referred as a velvet punch
The most intriguing comment heard yet
I'd sock you so sweet and taste like the greatest
hit
Just the tip of the tongue with a pinch
Approved

D'Villian

12

Grew up watching Baby James cut up at them
tiger games
Tigerettes ain't playing
And that Sonic Boom can break a tiger rest

Who are...

What would happen if social media crashed
We would be stuck as people
ITS alive

Let Us Limbo

14

I could love the Hell out of you
Share the Heaven in you if you let me

Ungrasp

15

Baby I got trust issues,
  last issue say he sold her stars boo
Could not fathom that constellation
With no consolation, I'd plant melted milky
ways in your pocket for when you fish for
another replacement

Intoxicated Curve

I knew I loved you when you spilt the beans
about digging the way my mind stream
First time an outsider ever had a clear gleam
In an attempt to not be overzealous, I made you
head or tails it
You guessed wrong and I ain't had to share it
If only I loved enough to the point of being
coherent
The dearest, was when you held me straight
them drunken nights

Tied

17

Around all these devices I'm feeling fried man
Put me on bread
I want to stick straight to the ribcage
But find myself by an outlet more frequent than
pleasant

Tide

18

Hold me down and I will keep us afloat

Hold me down and I will keep us afloat

Risk

We are stuck in love
Stuck in like we snuck in unaware of booby
traps
Tumbling, churning
Way before I even took a shot
A tumultuous existence
Eternal tides under moonlight
The Sun may never rise the way we cling to this
dream
Cloaked in feelings wishing to move
  the stars, the peak
No one better to trade for this galaxy we made
up

Watch Your Step

We found love...
In a hell infused rollercoaster made of cupcakes
It was frighteningly delicious
The quaking as it escalated made me shiver

A Unit

21

Coming to share only what I am
An iota, but noted
A singular beginning
Imaginary, still magical as ever

Ingram Content Group UK Ltd.
Milton Keynes UK
UKHW020707050623
422889UK00017B/2007